Happy Within
Feliz por dentro

By Marisa J. Taylor

Illustrated by Vanessa Balleza

BILINGUAL

English - Spanish

I love the color of my skin. I am unique and beautiful within.

Me encanta el color de mi piel, soy única y bonita tanto por dentro como por fuera.

I take pride in who I am and what I can do.

Estoy orgullosa de quien soy y de lo que puedo llegar a hacer.

Being me makes me happy from within.

Ser yo misma me hace feliz.

I love to sing, dance and play with my friends, but that is just me, that makes me happy.

Me encanta cantar, bailar y jugar con mis amigos, esto me hace feliz.

What about you? What makes you happy?

¿Y a ti? ¿Qué te hace feliz?

Some of my friends love to play with toys and make a lot of noise. That is okay too, because to them it brings joy.

A algunos de mis amigos les gusta hacer mucho ruido con los juguetes y eso les parece divertido.

Some of my friends love to sing, dance and chat away. That's okay, because everyone is different and special in their own way.

A algunos de mis amigos les encanta cantar, bailar y hablar cada segundo. Cada uno es diferente y especial en este mundo.

I do my best to be the best version of me.

Hago todo lo posible para ser la mejor versión de mi misma.

I do not compare myself to the other children
I see. I am proud of who I am and free to be me.

No me comparo con los otros niños que veo.
Estoy orgullosa de quien soy y de ser yo misma.

Some children will say things and make you feel sad.

Algunos niños dirán cosas sobre ti y te harán sentir triste.

Don't pay attention to their words and continue to be glad.

No les prestes atención a sus palabras y continúa estando alegre.

Let´s support one another to be the best we can be.

Animémonos y apoyémonos unos a otros para ser lo mejor que podamos ser.

Everyone is unique in their own special way.

Cada uno es único a su manera.

Be happy with who you are and what you see.

Sé feliz contigo mismo y con lo que tienes a tu alrededor.

It doesn't matter where in the world you are from, nor the color of your skin. BE YOU and do what makes you happy from within.

No importa de qué parte del mundo seas, ni el color de tu piel. Sé tú mismo y haz lo que te haga feliz.

The moment you feel the butterflies inside
and have a smile on your face,
do more of that to make you grin.

Cuando sientas las mariposas
en el estómago, párate y sonríe
y haz lo que te hace feliz.

One thing to remember
in order to be happy
from within...

Recuerda alguna cosa
que te haga feliz

Look at yourself in the mirror and say out loud "I am the best version of me and happy within my skin."

Mírate en el espejo y repite: Me siento cómodo en mi propia piel y soy la mejor versión de mi mismo.

If you believe in and love yourself, you can achieve anything and win.

Si crees en ti, puedes lograr cualquier cosa en la vida y ser feliz.

Being me makes me
Ser yo mismo(a) me hace....

. . . .

What about you?
What makes you happy?

¿Y a ti?
¿Qué te hace feliz?

LINGO BABIES

Happy Within
Feliz por dentro
Copyright © Lingo Babies, 2020

Written by Marisa J. Taylor
Illustrations: Vanessa Balleza

ISBN: 978-1-9163956-1-9

Graphic Design: Clementina Cortés
Spanish Translation: Elena Sosa

CPSIA information can be obtained
at www.ICGtesting.com
Printed in the USA
BVHW020442210821
614851BV00006B/515